NEW VANGUARD 348

US HEAVY TANKS OF WORLD WAR II

STEVEN J. ZALOGA   ILLUSTRATED BY FELIPE RODRÍGUEZ

OSPREY PUBLISHING

Bloomsbury Publishing Plc

Kemp House, Chawley Park, Cumnor Hill, Oxford OX2 9PH, UK

Bloomsbury Publishing Ireland Limited,

29 Earlsfort Terrace, Dublin 2, D02 AY28, Ireland

1385 Broadway, 5th Floor, New York, NY 10018, USA

E-mail: info@ospreypublishing.com

www.ospreypublishing.com

OSPREY is a trademark of Osprey Publishing Ltd

First published in Great Britain in 2026

A catalog record for this book is available from the British Library.

ISBN: PB 9781472870841; eBook 9781472870810; ePDF 9781472870827; XML 9781472870834

26 27 28 29 30 10 9 8 7 6 5 4 3 2 1

Index by Fionbar Lyons
Typeset by Lumina Datamatics Ltd
Printed by Repro India Ltd.

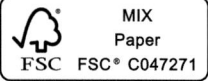

Title page caption

Please see caption on p. 7.

Osprey Publishing supports the Woodland Trust, the UK's leading woodland conservation charity.

To find out more about our authors and books visit www.ospreypublishing.com. Here you will find extracts, author interviews, details of forthcoming events and the option to sign up for our newsletter.

For product safety-related questions, contact productsafety@bloomsbury.com

Author's Note

The author would like to thank David Doyle for his help with the photos. All photos in this book, unless otherwise noted, are from official US government sources including the National Archives and Records Administration, the US Army Heritage and Education Center, the former Ordnance Museum at Aberdeen Proving Ground, and the Patton Museum at Fort Knox, Kentucky.

Glossary

AGF	Army Ground Forces; US Army branch responsible for organizing, training, and deploying army units
APG	Aberdeen Proving Ground, Maryland
ASF	Army Service Forces, branch of the US Army responsible for equipping army units
SHAEF	Supreme Headquarters Allied Expeditionary Force, Eisenhower's HQ
ton	short-ton, 2,000lb

CONTENTS

US HEAVY TANKS OF WORLD WAR II

INTRODUCTION

Why didn't the US Army field a heavy tank comparable to the German Tiger in World War II? The answer is that the US Army did develop a series of heavy tanks in World War II, but they remain largely unknown. Their obscurity is largely because few were built and fewer still went into combat. The reasons for this are the subject of this book.

The American Expeditionary Force in France in 1918 operated a battalion of British Mark V heavy tanks. These were successful enough that there was a joint US–UK program to manufacture the improved Mark VIII International tank for the battles anticipated in 1919. When the war ended in 1918, parts were available to assemble some of these even if the need had evaporated. Rock Island Arsenal completed 100 of these tanks between January and June 1920. The Mark VIII remained in service through the early 1930s. There was a scheme in 1932 to extend its life by replacing its engine with a more powerful Liberty aircraft engine. However, these tanks were obviously obsolete. Later in 1932, they were withdrawn from service and placed in storage.

The heavy tanks had not been popular in the inter-war years, especially with the Corps of Engineers. The Engineers complained that the Mark VIII was much too heavy for tactical bridging. This led to a decision in May 1936 to remove the designation "Heavy Tank" from the Ordnance Book of Standards, essentially eliminating the requirement for heavy tanks in the US Army.

The disappearance of US Army heavy tanks was short lived due to the outbreak of war in Europe. Following the German invasion of Poland, the Chief of Infantry, Maj. Gen. George Lynch, began discussions about a heavy tank with 2in or more of frontal armor. At the time, "heavy" meant any tank over 30 tons. Lynch saw the heavy tank as a special-purpose weapon, intended primarily to deal with enemy fortifications. Due to its size and weight, it was generally moved by railroad, except for short distances. Lynch's focus on the threat of fortifications was due to the extensive fortification network in Europe at the time, such as the French Maginot Line and the Siegfried Line, known as the Westwall in Germany.

With the German attacks on France in the spring of 1940, the Chief of Infantry began to outline the need for two types of heavy tanks. The smaller would be the same size as the existing M2 medium tank but with 3in of

The Mark VIII International tank was a cooperative Anglo-American venture to build a heavy tank for the 1919 campaign. This surviving example was preserved for many years at Aberdeen Proving Ground (APG).

frontal armor, a 75mm gun in the hull and a gun of 37mm to 50mm in a subsidiary turret. The larger of the two designs would be up to 80 tons with 3in of frontal armor, a hull-mounted gun in the 75mm to 105mm range, and a subsidiary turret mounting a gun in the 37mm to 50mm range, plus eight or more machine guns in various locations.

These concepts were influenced by the French Char B1 bis. It's worth noting that France had approached the United States government in 1940 about manufacturing the Hotchkiss H38, Somua S35 and Renault B1 bis, and had dispatched extensive information and drawings to the US Ordnance Department as the precursor of such a program. US military attachés in France had also been granted the opportunity to inspect a Char B1 bis tank unit in 1939.

Aside from French developments, the US Army's Military Intelligence Division had only sketchy information on other foreign heavy tanks. Over the years, military attachés in Moscow had photographed the Soviet T-35 heavy tank at military parades. Film footage had appeared of the experimental Soviet T-100 and SMK multi-turret tanks in Finland in 1940. A more alarming development was the appearance of an unknown German tank during the invasion of Norway in April 1940. Technical details of this multi-turret tank were not known at the time, but there were rumors of German tanks of 70 tons or more. In fact, the Norwegian mystery tank was the Neubaufahrzeug, a failed tank that was used by the Wehrmacht for propaganda purposes.

M6 (T1) HEAVY TANKS

Following the invasion of France in May 1940, the Chief of Infantry issued a formal requirement to the Ordnance Department for a new heavy tank in the 50 to 80-ton range. The requirements document noted that "The recent rapid development of antitank guns and mechanized vehicles armed with

The T1E2 heavy tank pilot shortly after delivery to APG, February 28, 1942.

The T1E2 pilot was originally fitted with an external exhaust and muffler system. It was replaced with an internal system before the tank was delivered for trials. This view also shows the T50 anti-aircraft rotor mount on the right rear corner of the turret and the T51 cupola mount.

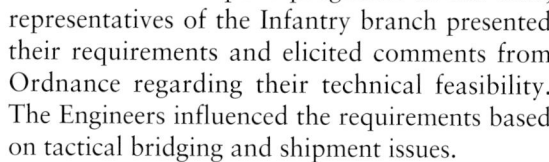

weapons of 75mm and larger calibers has created a demand for a heavily armored and armed tank."

The initial scheme for a heavy tank based on the existing M2 medium tank quickly evolved into the M3 medium tank, leaving only the larger heavy tank design outstanding. Ordnance had already begun to make some preliminary sketches of possible designs. The general characteristics of the new heavy tank were approved at an Ordnance Committee Meeting on May 22, 1940, although a final design had not yet been developed.

The Ordnance Committee brought together members of the various combat and service branches to coordinate new weapons programs. In this case, representatives of the Infantry branch presented their requirements and elicited comments from Ordnance regarding their technical feasibility. The Engineers influenced the requirements based on tactical bridging and shipment issues.

Details of the May 1940 meeting are lacking. No doubt Engineer concern over the weight and size of the new heavy tank must have been overruled by the Infantry due to the gravity of the war situation in Europe. Although the US was not yet at war, there was general recognition in Washington that there was a high probability that the US Army would be dragged into the conflict sooner or later. This provided the urgency for the development of new tanks.

The initial scheme for the new heavy tank had been drawn up by Ordnance and anticipated a tank 50 tons in weight and 25ft in length. The width was restricted to 9ft to permit railroad transport. Armor protection was 3in (76mm) in front, and 2.5in (65mm) on the sides. These were unremarkable, but the layout of the proposal was extravagant: two turrets armed with the

75mm T6 gun, two secondary turrets with 20mm and 37mm guns with co-axial .30-cal. machine guns, and four more .30-cal. machine guns in the front hull. Ordnance was familiar with multi-turret designs, since most inter-war light tanks were fitted with twin machine gun turrets. However, the idea of a tank with four turrets was ostentatious. Sadly, none of the drawings of this configuration appear to have survived. The concept for the new heavy tank was probably influenced by foreign designs, such as the Soviet T-35 that had a 76mm gun turret, two 45mm gun turrets, and two machine gun turrets. The requirements were approved on July 11, 1940 and the new vehicle designated as the T1 heavy tank.

This front view of the T1E2 pilot shows the proliferation of machine guns, including two .30 cals in T53 mounts in the bow corners, a pair of .50-cal. machine guns in the T52 twin mount in the hull front, and a .30-cal. in the traversable T51 cupola on the turret roof.

The multi-turret concept was short-lived. On July 10, 1940, the Armored Force was created and became responsible for oversight of tank development instead of the Infantry. This helped clear away the Infantry's penchant for tanks bristling with multiple turrets and machine guns. With their hands freed from Infantry influence, Ordnance revised the design into a more conventional layout with a single turret armed with a 3in T12 gun. Curiously, the 3in gun was paired with a co-axial 37mm M5 gun in a T49 combination mount. The 37mm gun was not a secondary weapon. The ammunition stowage for the 37mm gun was an impressive 202 rounds. Its main function was to deal with enemy machine gun nests, while the more powerful 3in gun was available for more substantial fortifications. The T12 3in gun was subsequently standardized as the M7.

The subsidiary turrets of the original design disappeared, but there was still a significant amount of secondary firepower. In the hull front were no fewer than four machine guns: two .50-cal. machine guns in the right front superstructure in a T52 twin mount operated by a dedicated bow gunner, and two .30-cal. machine guns on either corner of the bow in T53 mounts with limited elevation control. These latter two machine guns were operated by the driver, a common feature on US light and medium tanks of the day. On the series-production tanks, the two lower hull machine guns were reduced to one. On the upper right corner of the turret was an awkward T50 rotor mount for a .50-cal. anti-aircraft machine gun. It is very hard to see how such a mount could be used to track and engage a fast-moving aircraft. It was deleted on the series-production tanks.

The T1 heavy tank was heavily influenced by the French Somua S35 in terms of shape and construction, though considerably larger. It adopted the French preference for cast hulls and turrets to simplify production, even though no US tank to this point had made extensive use of casting. The layout was similar to the Somua tank with a narrow hull and a correspondingly high superstructure with a large engine compartment.

Due to the size and weight of the T1 heavy tank, the Baldwin Locomotive Works (BLW) was selected in August 1940 to construct a pilot model to be

An interior view of the turret of the M6 heavy tank showing the T49 combination mount consisting of an M7 3in gun on the right and the M6 37mm gun on the left.

A cross-sectional view of the M6A2 (T1E1). The size of the tank was in part dictated by the large size of its Wright G-200 engine and General Electric drive motors, and associated electric generator.

followed by 50 production tanks. BLW was headquartered in Eddystone, Pennsylvania, as was General Steel Castings, the firm assigned the task of creating the cast armor for the hull and turret. A wooden sub-scale model of the T1 heavy tank was built and displayed. The revised design was presented at the October 24, 1940 Ordnance Committee Meeting and formally approved on November 22, 1940.

A rationale for a heavy tank was presented in an article by Capt. C.R. Kutz, "Break-Through Tanks: Will They Bring Freedom of Action to Armored Divisions?" in the November 1940 issue of *Army Ordnance* magazine. Kutz suggested that the surprising use of heavy breakthrough tanks in the 1940 Battle of France was one of the reasons for Germany's victory. In his view, French and British light tanks had been overmatched by German medium and heavy tanks. He concluded by arguing that "Only the break-through tank, properly combined with other arms, can stop hostile penetration or effect a break-through and ensure freedom of action to armored divisions." Kutz's ill-informed article revealed the underlying shortcomings of the US Army's technical intelligence at the time that hampered efforts to anticipate future battlefield threats.

By 1940 and 1941 standards, the T1 heavy tank was mediocre. It was better than Britain's archaic TOG heavy tank.[1] However, it did not compare well to the Soviet Union's new KV-1 that had already entered production late in 1940. Germany's VK 30.01 (H), the predecessor to the Tiger, was not as well armored with a maximum of 65mm, but it was much lighter at only 32 metric tons. In 1940–41, the American tank program suffered from having too many projects being developed with too little engineering talent. This wasn't rectified until well into 1942, when America's considerable engineering talent in the automotive and railroad industry were brought to bear on the problem.

The weight of the T1 heavy tank raised eyebrows, since no previous US tank had approached 50 tons. This implied the need for a powerplant in the 1,000hp range. As a result, Ordnance turned to the Society of Automotive Engineers (SAE) for advice. An SAE special committee considered existing automotive and aviation engines and suggested the Allison V-1710 in-line aircraft engine, the Wright G-200 radial aircraft engine, and a General Motors diesel.

1   See: Kenneth Estes, *Super-Heavy Tanks of World War II*, Osprey New Vanguard 216: 2014.

The Allison was ruled out, since the aviation industry had preference for this powerplant. Ultimately, the Wright G-200 was selected, as it offered 960 gross horsepower at 2,300rpm.

The next major technical problem to emerge, and one that would trouble the T1 heavy tank throughout its life, was the choice of a suitable transmission for such a powerful engine. No automobile or truck transmission could handle the power of the Wright G-200. An SAE committee recommended investigating torque converters from Schneider Hydraulic Corp., the Twin Disc Clutch Co., and Borg Warner Corp. Another solution was the new Hydramatic transmission proposed by the Oldsmobile Division of General Motors. There were also suggestions that electric drives, as used in locomotives, should be considered, with the Electromotive Division of General Motors and General Electric cited. Initially, electric drives were ruled out due to weight. Ordnance selected the new Hydramatic transmission as its first choice with torque converters as a possible substitute.

In the event, problems developing a suitable transmission forced Ordnance to proceed with several versions of the T1 tank from the beginning. The basic T1 heavy tank designation applied to a tank with the Hydramatic transmission. The February 13, 1941 Ordnance Committee Meeting approved a proposal to build a T1E1 pilot with a new electric transmission after General Electric demonstrated that it was only two tons heavier than conventional mechanical transmissions. When the schedule to deliver the Hydramatic transmission in May 1941 proved unobtainable, Ordnance added the T1E2 pilot with a Twin Disc Model T-16001 torque converter linking the engine to a conventional mechanical transmission.

BLW worked on pilots for three configurations during the second half of 1941, completing the T1E2 pilot in September. At the time of the Japanese attack on Pearl Harbor on December 7, 1941, only the T1E2 pilot was ready for testing. It was delivered to Aberdeen Proving Ground (APG) in Maryland in February 1942 after its original engine exhaust system had been extensively modified, due to problems uncovered during initial factory trials in 1941.

America's entry into World War II added pressure to put the T1 heavy tank into mass production. As was the case with the M3 and M4 medium tanks, Ordnance decided to develop a welded-hull version of the T1E2, designated as T1E3, as a back-up for the cast hull version. No pilot of the welded hull T1E3 was deemed necessary, although a single T1E3/M6A1 was built by the Fisher Body Division of General Motors in 1943 as an "educational" example to broaden the potential production base. In the event, no further production by Fisher was undertaken for reasons that will become evident below.

The G-200 radial engine used in the T1 heavy tank was a variant of the R-1820 aircraft engine that powered types such as the B-17 bomber and C-47 transport. Since the aircraft received higher industrial priority, Ordnance decided to add a back-up powerplant on the proposed T1E4 consisting of four GM 6-71 bus engines combined in a single powerpack. In the event, this version was never built.

T1 heavy tank variants				
Test designation	Transmission	Engine	Hull	Service designation
T1	Hydramatic	G-200	cast	canceled
T1E1	GE electric	G-200	cast	M6A2
T1E2	Torque converter	G-200	cast	M6
T1E3	Torque converter	G-200	welded	M6A1
T1E4	Torque converter	4 × GM 6-71 diesel	cast	canceled

Due to the shortage of tanks for the new US Army armored divisions, BLW was awarded an initial contract for the production of eight T1E2 heavy tanks in December 1941. This was followed shortly by an order for 12 T1E3 heavy tanks. On April 12, 1942, the Ordnance Committee Meeting recommended standardizing the T1E2 as the M6 heavy tank and the T1E3 as the M6A1 heavy tank; this was rubber stamped by the Army Adjutant General on May 26, 1942.

In January 1942, President Franklin Roosevelt sent a letter to the Secretary of War outlining weapons production goals over the next two years. It called for the manufacture of 500 heavy tanks in 1942 and 5,000 in 1943. This was regarded as wildly unrealistic by Ordnance. The total production objective in the spring of 1942 was 1,084 heavy tanks.

The initial production M6A1 at the General Motors Proving Ground in January 1943, showing the welded-hull configuration that distinguished it from the M6 heavy tank.

Another driver for US tank production at this time was the British and Soviet requirements for tanks via the Lend–Lease program. The M6 was never offered to the Soviet Union, and the initial British request was modest, 150 tanks with a total objective sometimes put at 500 tanks. The British Tank Mission in the US regarded the T1 heavy tank as a stopgap until the T14 assault tank was ready, as described below. A British assessment of the T1 heavy tank was contained in a February 1942 report by the Tank Mission in Washington, DC that supervised Anglo-American programs:

> [The T1 heavy tank] was a marvelous conception for a tank which would be required in limited numbers only on account of transportation difficulties. The 3-inch gun and good armour with reasonable speed should make it a formidable fighting weapon. Some trouble has been encountered with the steering which we feel is the weakest point in the design of such a heavy tank. We are trying to get a .30 Browning MG mounted co-axially alongside the 3-inch and 37mm guns in the turret, but this may not be possible. Some people feel they would like to dispense with the 37mm gun and fit two MGs instead. When, however, the enormous size of the 3-inch round is seen, one appreciates the wisdom of having the 37mm. We regard this tank as ideal for fighting enemy tanks and not for chasing infantry.

The development of the M6 heavy tank was hampered by the immaturity of its powertrain and the need to develop manufacturing techniques for its large cast hull. From the start of its development in May 1940 to the first series production tank in December 1942 was 32 months. In contrast, the M3 medium tank, based on the mature M2A1 medium tank, took only 13 months from inception to first serial production in June 1941.

Testing of the T1E2 Pilot No.1 found that the powertrain "provided adequate power," but it discovered that the Hycon hydraulic steering system was prone to failure. This led to the installation of a vacuum-mechanical steering system that proved more reliable. Numerous other changes were introduced including the substitution of a twin GM 3700 Torqmatic transmission with a three-speed gear box for the original Twin Disc T-16000

An overhead view of the sole M6A1 tank built by Fisher showing its welded hull configuration.

An M6A2 heavy tank fitted with a T7 90mm gun on display at a public exhibit in Washington, DC in February 1944 during a war-bond drive.

torque converter with a two-speed gear box. However, the shortcomings in contemporary transmission technology undermined the T1 program. The T1E1 had a nominal gross horsepower of 960hp, but a net horsepower of only about 700hp.

In early 1942, there was a study to increase the armor on the T1 heavy tank to 5in (127mm) on the front, 4in (101mm) on the turret, and 3in (76mm) on the sides with a potential overall weight increase of 9,500lb. This was supported by the British Tank Mission, but it was not approved by Ordnance.

Although the T1/M6 heavy tank formally entered series production in 1942, its troubles were only beginning, due to the change in management of the tank programs. The T1 heavy tank had been created while the Infantry branch still directed tank programs. When the Armored Force was created in July 1940, requirements for the tank programs were taken out of Infantry hands. The new leadership of the Armored Force, such as Gen. Adna Chaffee, were from the Cavalry branch. The Cavalry had never been fond of the Infantry's multi-turreted tanks, and generally preferred mobility over armored protection. In early 1942, the Germans had not yet fielded a long 75mm or 88mm tank gun, and the armor of medium tanks such as the M4 Sherman seemed perfectly adequate. As far as firepower was concerned, the 3in gun on the M6 heavy tank was also being mounted on the M10 3in Gun Motor Carriage, a derivative of the M4 tank that entered production in September 1942. A 76mm gun was also being experimentally mounted in the M4A1 Sherman medium tank. These factors reduced the appeal of the M6 heavy tank to the Armored Force.

Armored Force planning in 1941 did not include a specific role for heavy tanks, and no Table of Organization & Equipment (TO&E) for a heavy tank battalion was drawn up. With no M6 heavy tanks available in the summer of 1942 for operational trials, the Armored Force became increasingly indifferent to the new tank. Although the Armored Force blamed technical flaws in the powertrain uncovered during 1942 testing, in reality they saw no need for such a heavy tank and recognized the difficulties they would face trying to transport such a vehicle overseas to the combat theaters. Furthermore, the M6 heavy tank was quite expensive, costing about $170,000 compared to about $45,000 for an M4 Sherman medium tank, nearly four times the cost.

In June 1942, the development program for the T1 heavy tank project was trimmed back. Further work on the baseline T1 was canceled and the General

1

2

3

Motors Hydramatic transmission was never installed in a tank. The T1E4 with its multiple diesel engines was also canceled. Early testing of the pilot tanks favored the GE electric transmission of the T1E1 over the torque-converter transmission in the M6 and M6A1. Despite this, the T1E1 was never formally standardized as the M6A2 as had been planned. Nevertheless, the designation M6A2 was widely used in Army documents from 1942 to 1945 and it will be used here, even though it was only a provisional designation.

The short-term procurement objective for the M6 heavy tank series was increased from 115 to 230 tanks under the May 1942 program with the plan being for 50 M6, 65 M6A1 and 115 M6A2 tanks. Army Services of Supply decided that the M6 and M6A1 tanks would be delivered to the UK under Lend–Lease while the US Army would receive the M6A2.

The fate of the M6 program abruptly changed on December 7, 1942 when Maj. Gen. Jacob Devers, commander of the Armored Forces, informed Lt Gen. Lesley McNair, commander of Army Ground Forces (AGF), that "Due to its tremendous weight and limited tactical use, there is no requirement in the Armored Force for the heavy tank. The increase in the power of the armament of the heavy tank does not compensate for the heavier armor." Devers noted that it would be preferable to use the available shipping to transport two M4 Sherman medium tanks overseas rather than a single M6 heavy tank. The November 1942 amphibious landings on the French North African coast for Operation *Torch* had highlighted the difficulties of landing tanks, even medium tanks. The M3 and M4 medium tanks had to be off-loaded from transport ships using dockside cranes after the ports had been captured.

McNair concurred with Devers and, as a result, the Services of Supply directed the termination of production of the M6 heavy tank beyond those already being constructed under existing contracts. Plans to form two heavy tank battalions to use the M6A2 tank were canceled. A March 1943 Ordnance Committee determined the minimum economical number to be 40 tanks, as detailed in the accompanying chart. This would bring total production to 43 tanks including the three pilots. The first series production M6 was not delivered from BLW until December 1942, with tanks dribbling off the assembly lines at a snail's pace until completed in February 1944. Although there had been plans to send an M6 heavy tank to the UK for trials in September 1942, the slow rate of construction and the eventual cancelation of the program meant that the UK never received any M6 heavy tanks.

M6 tank production

	M6	M6A1	M6A2
Dec 42	1		
Jan 43			
Feb 43			
Mar 43	3		
Apr 43	1		
May 43	2		1
Jun 43		1	1
Jul 43	1		2
Aug 43		2	2
Sep 43		3	2
Oct 43		4	2
Nov 43		1	3
Dec 43		1	3
Jan 44			3
Feb 44			1
Total	**8**	**12**	**20**

M6 production tanks

Type	Quantity	Registration no.	Serial no.
M6	8	308957–308964	3 to 10
M6A1	12	3014164–3014172	11 to 22
M6A2	20	3094306–3094325	23 to 42

The delivery of the first serial production tanks led to extensive testing. Trials of a production M6A1 tank at the GM Proving Ground in Milford, Michigan found "No major deficiency [only] minor faults were listed." However, subsequent Army tests of production M6 and M6A1 tanks were scathing. A July 1943 report concluded that "The test tanks were not considered satisfactory because of inadequate and obsolete fire control equipment; insufficient ventilation for the fighting compartment; an unsatisfactory transmission; and poor positioning of controls, crew, and seats." The only use of the M6 heavy tanks by the Armored Force was by a single heavy tank company established at Fort Knox in 1943 to assist the Armored Board to conduct operational trials. Some tanks were also sent to the Yuma Test Branch of the Engineer Board of the Corps of Engineers at Imperial Dam, Arizona to test heavy engineer bridging.

Ordnance hoped that by increasing the firepower of the M6 heavy tank, the Armored Force would change its opinion about its combat value. In March 1943, the T1E1 pilot tank was fitted with the T7 90mm gun, derived from the 90mm anti-aircraft gun. This proved satisfactory in test firing, though Ordnance did acknowledge that turret redesign would be needed.

One of the principal objections to the M6 heavy tank was the lack of suitable tactical bridging. This is an experiment with M6 serial number 3, the first production M6, on a trestle bridge at the Yuma Test Branch of the Engineer Board of the Corps of Engineers at Imperial Dam, Arizona, March 1944.

An interesting size comparison of the M6A2 heavy tank next to a M4A1 (76mm) at APG. (Author)

At least one production M6A2 was fitted with a 90mm gun and it saw extensive public display in 1944 during the 5th War Bond Drive. The new 90mm gun did not change the viewpoint of the Armored Force, since at this stage, there was no need seen for such a powerful gun.

Prior to the Normandy landings in June 1944, the Armored Section of SHAEF (Supreme Headquarters Allied Expeditionary Force) had been pressing Ordnance for the supply of vehicles suitable for engaging German bunkers on the Siegfried Line. The outcome of this request led to the development of the M36 90mm Gun Motor Carriage, the M4A3E2 assault tank, and the refurbishment of the M12 155mm Gun Motor Carriage. Ordnance also offered to modify 15 M6A2 tanks as assault tanks. This involved the increase of the front hull armor to 7.5in (190mm) and the addition of a new turret with the experimental T5E1 105mm gun. AGF opposed this effort, arguing that the M6 would have to be completely updated. AGF was so fed up with Ordnance's promotion of half-baked schemes for the M6 that in July 1944, they recommended that it be declared obsolete. Ordnance managed to deflect this recommendation for the time being.

The Ordnance Committee Meeting on August 14, 1944 authorized a 105mm gun conversion as the M6A2E1 with an initial delivery by November 15, 1944. AGF was indifferent to the proposal, so Army Service Forces (ASF) referred the matter to SHAEF in Europe. Eisenhower's headquarters responded on August 18, 1944 that it considered the M6A2E1 impractical for the European Theater of Operations (ETO), so it canceled the project, aside from the two pilots. Ordnance continued with the project into 1945, justifying the M6A2E1 pilots as testbeds for the forthcoming T29 heavy tank that was armed with the same 105mm gun. It was test-fired at APG, Maryland in 1945.

Trials at APG disclosed that the new turret increased the weight of the M6A2E1 to 77 tons. This adversely affected automotive performance and the tanks could not negotiate a 40 percent slope. The latter has 4 units of vertical rise for each 10 units of horizontal distance or roughly equivalent to 22 degrees. This would have significantly limited the mobility of the M6A2E1 in the ETO, since it would have been stopped by modest hills. AGF deprecated the design, pointing out that it could not proceed to the battlefront under its own power except through "a combination of most unusual, unexpected, and fortunate events" and that it could not be transported by other means such as railroad or tank transporters due to its excessive weight and width.

The December 1944 Ordnance Committee Meeting finally declared the M6 heavy tanks to be obsolete. They were shipped to Rock Island Arsenal, where they were subsequently scrapped. A single M6A2 and one of the M6A2E1 pilots were preserved at the Ordnance Museum at APG. However, the M6A2E1 was scrapped during the Korean War.

Heavy tanks of 1943–44 size comparison (right to left): US T14, German Tiger I, US M6A1.

Overall, the M6 heavy tank program was a flop. It was a mediocre design based on an outdated 1940 view of battlefield requirements. The long delay in its development meant that it did not reach production until 1943, by which time far more modern heavy tanks, such as the Tiger I, had already reached the battlefield.

Heavy tank comparison: 1943

Type	M6A2	Tiger I	T14
Crew	6	5	5
Weight (tons: unloaded)	60.3	60	42.6
Length (ft)	27.7	27.7	20.3
Width (ft)	10.3	12.1	10.4
Height (ft)	9.8	9.6	11.4
Engine (hp)	960	690	520
Hp/ton ratio	15.9	11.5	12.9
Ground pressure (psi)	13.1	10.0	11.3
Road speed (mph)	20	28	24
Main gun (mm)	76	88	75
Turret frontal armor (mm)	102	100	102
Turret side armor (mm)	83	80	102
Hull frontal armor (mm)	83	100	89
Hull side armor (mm)	70	60	76

T14 ASSAULT TANK

The T14 assault tank was the only US Army tank design from World War II that was solely designed for another army. Informal discussions were held between the staff of the British Tank Mission in Washington, DC and Ordnance officers in late 1941 about the possibility of developing a more heavily armored version of the M4 Sherman as a potential candidate for a British heavy infantry tank. Production of such a tank was already

The T14 Pilot No. 1 on trials at APG, 1943.

underway in Britain as the A22 Churchill. However, the A22 program was plagued with technical problems and there was some concern it would be canceled. A January 1942 report complained that, at any given time, 42 percent of the Churchills were nonfunctional due to technical problems.

The American program was initiated on February 21, 1942 as a result of discussions in Washington, DC between US Army Ordnance and a British delegation from London, including senior leaders from the Ministry of Supply and the War Office. After explaining the problems with the Churchill infantry tank, British officials inquired as to whether a "heavier edition" of the US M4 Sherman tank might be a better solution. This discussion was continued on March 30, 1942 between Lt Gen. Sir Gordon N. Macready, the head of the British Army mission in Washington along with British Tank Mission members and senior Ordnance Department officials. Macready formally requested that Ordnance develop an infantry tank for British use. It was described as a heavily armored, low-silhouette vehicle with low ground pressure, moderate speed and using as many components of the M4 medium tank as possible. The objective would be to manufacture 8,500 of these infantry tanks in the US for Lend–Lease supply to Britain.

There had already been some preliminary design work on this concept at APG in late 1941 with the general preference for a new design using M4 components rather than an up-armored M4 medium tank. This was based on the presumption that the added armor weight could not be accommodated by the Sherman's suspension or powertrain. The basic characteristics called for armor of 3in (76mm) on the hull, 4in (106mm) on the turret, and the same 75mm gun as the Sherman. The gun mounting would be adaptable to the British 6pdr gun. In July 1942, Ordnance decided to study alternative armament mountings including the 76mm gun, the 90mm gun, and the 105mm howitzer. The weight was expected to be 46 tons with a top speed of 18mph using a Ford GAZ V-8 engine and the existing Sherman tank drivetrain. The program was formally approved as the T14 assault tank at an Ordnance Committee meeting on May 14, 1942. The designation "assault tank" was an American equivalent of the British infantry tank designation and was chosen to distinguish the program from the T1/M6 heavy tank. There was hesitancy to use the term "infantry tank," since this might be confused with the pre-war distinction between US infantry tanks and cavalry combat cars. There were expectations that the T14 would be ready for production by the summer of 1943.

B

T14 ASSAULT TANK, US ARMY ARMORED BOARD, FORT KNOX, KENTUCKY, 1944

The one and only T14 assault tank in US Army service was dispatched to Fort Knox in 1943 for trials by the Armored Board there. The Armored Board assigned a test number to each tank that was painted on the turret and hull. Nicknames were uncommon on Armored Board tanks, but this was obviously an exception. Otherwise, it is finished in the standard lusterless olive drab with blue drab registration number.

1

2

3

The initial program included the construction of two pilots at the ALCO (American Locomotive) plant in Schenectady, New York. A wooden mock-up arrived in Schenectady in July 1942 to guide the manufacturing process. It took about a year to build the two pilots with the first arriving at APG for trials on July 29, 1943 and the second on August 26, 1943.

Although the Armored Force had no requirement for such a vehicle, in July 1943, Fort Knox requested that a T14 assault tank be shipped to the center as soon as possible to compare it with the M6 heavy tanks undergoing operational trials there. Ordnance was reluctant to transfer either of the pilots to Fort Knox until some minimal testing was completed. Likewise, the pilot intended for Britain was also tested before shipment.

The second pilot of the T14 assault tank was shipped to the UK in 1944 and is seen here during trials.

The testing at APG was completed on December 3, 1943 and uncovered the usual number of technical problems encountered in new tank designs. A report written at the time concluded that "based on the test performed at Aberdeen Proving Ground, it is concluded that the Assault Tank T14, in its present state of development, is unsatisfactory because of the deficiencies [listed here]." The air cleaners were inaccessible for servicing and excessively exposed to dirt and dust. The brakes required excessive action to operate. There was inadequate ventilation in the turret when the 75mm gun was firing. There were numerous problems with engine fittings and the fuel system. The suspension was vulnerable to damage, the tracks were thrown frequently, and it was difficult to adjust track tension. Most of these problems were redeemable. However, by the time that the T14 assault tank was ready, the requirement had evaporated.

T14 Pilot No. 2 in the UK showing the side skirts open to reveal the suspension. The bogies were derived from those used on the M6 heavy tank.

When British officials had requested the development of the T14 in March 1942, the Churchill infantry tank was immature. However, by the summer of 1943, the Churchill was a seasoned design and widely committed to combat. The T14 assault tank offered no exceptional advances over the Churchill, and furthermore, the British equivalent to the T14, the A33 Excelsior, was also in testing.

The T14 Pilot No. 1 was shipped to Fort Knox in

mid-December 1943 for operational testing. The T14 Pilot No. 2 was shipped to the Chester Tank Depot in mid-December 1943 on its way to the UK. On arriving in the UK, the T14 was subjected to testing through April 1945, even though any plans to order the tank via Lend–Lease had long since been discarded. The T14 assault tank program was formally closed on December 14, 1945, but it had been effectively dead since the end of 1943.

Heavy tank comparison: 1944			
Type	M6A2E1	Tiger II	M26
Crew	5	5	5
Weight (tons: unloaded)	73.5	75.5	42.4
Length (ft)	36.7	33.8	28.3
Width (ft)	10.3	12.3	11.5
Height (ft)	11.4	10.1	9.9
Engine (hp)	960	690	500
Hp/ton ratio	13.1	9.1	11.8
Ground pressure (hp/t)	15.9	10.8	12.5
Road speed (mph)	18	25.8	30
Main gun	105	88	90
Turret frontal armor (mm)	191	180	114
Turret side armor (mm)	89	80	101
Hull frontal armor (mm)	191	150	101
Hull side armor (mm)	70	80	76

Heavy tanks of 1944 size comparison (right to left): US M6A2E1, German Tiger II, US M26 Pershing.

M4A3E2 ASSAULT TANK

In January 1944, officers of the Armored Section, European Theater of Operations–US Army (ETOUSA) in London submitted an urgent requirement to Washington for 250 heavy tanks for the upcoming campaign in France. They anticipated the need for tanks with thicker armor when confronting the German Siegfried Line defenses.

The Ordnance Department had foreseen the potential need for an "extra heavy" Sherman with additional armor. This revived the 1941 British idea of a "Heavy M4" that had led to the T14 assault tank. On December 17, 1943, Ordnance instructed the General Motors Proving Ground to modify an M4A3 tank with ballast to bring its test weight to 41.3 tons and to conduct a 500-mile automotive trial over the standard endurance course. The test tank was

The M4A3E2 assault tank was based on the normal Sherman medium tank with substantially thicker armor. Chrysler developed the new D7067403 turret that was similar in size to the turret used with the 76mm gun, but with thicker armor. This particular tank with turret number 8 was tested by the Armored Board at Fort Knox in February 1944. It later served as the basis for the T33 flamethrower tank pilot.

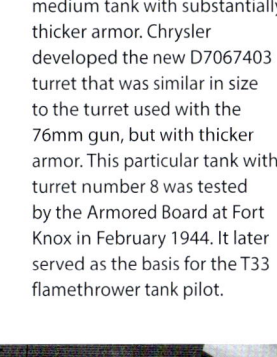

fitted with extended end connectors on the track that reduced the ground pressure to 14.2lb per square inch. Trials started in January 1944 and General Motors concluded that "no abnormal failures were encountered ... therefore, [it] appears feasible to convert a Medium Tank into an Assault Tank ... if only limited operation is to be encountered."

In February 1944, the Development Division of the US AGF concurred that a heavily armored assault tank would be needed in the upcoming campaign in Europe to deal with fortified German objectives. Since the new T26E2 (Pershing) heavy tank was not expected to be ready for many months, an expedient design based around an up-armored M4A3 medium tank was recommended by the Armored Branch. As an alternative, Ordnance proposed that the M6 heavy tank could be modified for the role. The AGF strongly opposed the M6 option due to the many problems that were revealed during M6 testing. These issues were settled in early March 1944, in favor of the M4 assault tank, which was renamed the M4A3E2.

Gen. Gladeon Barnes, the Ordnance Department's Chief of Research and Engineering, was not entirely happy with this concept. His diary on March 2, 1944 noted that "We need [the M4A3E2], because we have been held up on the heavier tanks, and this is a stop gap. This M4 tank has the armor of the heavy tank and is very much overloaded. General Barnes is going to try to see that no more of these are built."

The M4A3E2 differed from the normal M4A3 medium tank in several respects. The M4A3E2 used a new turret with 6in (152mm) armor in place of the normal turret. It was fitted with the T110 combination mount. This mount was developed from the T80 combination gun mount developed for the 76mm M1 tank gun. Although the M4A3E2 was fitted with the standard 75mm M3 tank gun, the T110 mount allowed it to be readily adapted to the 76mm gun if the need arose. A new final drive casting was fitted on the bow with 5.5in (140mm) of armor. Additional armor plates 1.5in thick (38mm) were welded to the glacis and sides. Since this increased the tank's weight to 42 tons, extended end connectors were fitted to the track as used in the General Motors tests. The Army approved a production run

C **M4A3E2 ASSAULT TANK**

1. M4A3E2 Assault Tank, B Company, 68th Tank Battalion, 6th Armored Division, Germany, 1945. "Blue Eyes" had its blue drab registration numbers and yellow transport markings overpainted with more visible white numbers. The registration number was used daily for maintenance purposes, so many units preferred them to be more visible than the standard army regulation low-visibility style. "Blue Eyes" also had the name "Miss Persuader" painted on the gun barrel. The 68th Tank Battalion sometimes used a cartoon "Battling Turtle" insignia, but this does not appear to have been applied when this M4A3E2 replaced the original "Blue Eyes" M4 tank in October 1944. The bumper code is in the usual fashion with division and battalion on the right side, and the company and tank number on the left.

2. M4A3E2 (76mm), A Company, 15th Tank Battalion, 6th Armored Division, Germany, 1945. "Aquino" was re-armed with a 76mm gun in early 1945 as part of a Third US Army program. The registration number has been locally repainted in large white numbers, since the factory-applied blue drab registration numbers were too faint to read or had been overpainted during shipment. The 15th Tank Battalion used a wolf's head insignia as well as large white "speed-numbers" as a method to more quickly identify tanks in combat. Many Sherman tanks in the 6th Armored Division had a length of steel bar welded to the upper turret sides to make it easier for the crew to stow their gear on the outside of the tank. "Aquino" was finished in the usual overall lusterless olive drab.

1

2

The M4A3E2 could take a terrible amount of punishment. This assault tank of the 743rd Tank Battalion was knocked out near Fronhoven in late November 1944 after having been hit by four 88mm rounds from an anti-tank gun about 800yds away near Lohn. One bounced off the glacis plate and two off the mantlet before a lucky hit was made that entered the telescope opening. This tank was fitted with an E4-5 flamethrower in the hull machine gun position.

of 250 assault tanks, which would be available by August 1944. The design was completed on a rush basis and the first 40 were manufactured at the Grand Blanc tank arsenal in May, and the remaining tanks through July 1944 with a total of 254 being manufactured.

A total of 250 M4A3E2 assault tanks were released to the ETO on August 29, 1944. They first began arriving in France in September and the first batch of 54 was issued to the First US Army in mid-October. As of late October 1944, 105 were destined for the First US Army, 90 to the Third US Army, and 60 to the Ninth US Army. In fact, delivery was much slower than expected, and by the end of November there had been only 140 issued to units. The remainder of the tanks were delivered gradually, and a small number were diverted for the Seventh US Army in Alsace.

There was no tactical doctrine for assault tanks in the US Army and the armor officers in the ETO headquarters concluded that such tanks would be more useful in the separate tank battalions attached to infantry divisions. For example, in Patton's Third Army in late November 1944, there were only five with the 10th Armored Division, but there were 15 with the 737th Tank Battalion, and five each in the 702nd, 712th, 735th, and 761st Tank Battalions. At first, several of Patton's armored division commanders did not see any need for an assault tank, including respected tank commanders such as John P. Wood of 4th Armored Division and Robert W. Grow of 6th Armored Division. But as the battlefield became soaked by autumn rains, the soggy terrain "narrowed the front to a width only one tank wide." As a result, the Germans were able to concentrate their anti-tank guns on predictable routes and stymie US tank advances. Under these circumstances, the armored division commanders changed their minds and began pleading for the assault tanks. In December, the late-arriving assault tanks were issued to armored divisions.

The 4th Armored Division received several assault tanks prior to its mission in late December to relieve the 101st Airborne Division, which was trapped in Bastogne by the German Ardennes offensive. The lead tank of Patton's drive on Bastogne was an M4A3E2 of Company C, 37th Tank Battalion, commanded by Lt Charles Boggess, nicknamed Cobra King. Boggess was awarded the Silver Star for bravery during the fighting for the town of Cobreville on Christmas Day. Cobra King was the first US tank from Patton's relief effort to enter Bastogne on December 26, 1944. Curiously enough, this tank survived the war and is now displayed at the National Museum of the US Army at Fort Belvoir, Virginia.

The M4A3E2 assault tanks were an immediate success with the tankers. During the wet autumn months of 1944, the US Army was bogged down in savage fighting along the German Westwall defenses. In spite of their added weight, the tank crews found that the M4A3E2 assault tanks were about as maneuverable as the normal M4 medium tanks. Their main appeal, of course, was their thick armor, which was sufficient to resist direct frontal hits from the 88mm gun at typical combat ranges. Most tanks knocked out by enemy action were due to hits on the sides. On receiving an enquiry about the assault tanks from headquarters, the chief of staff of Patton's Third Army reported that "Everyone wants the M4A3E2." In fact, the M4A3E2 proved so popular that the commander of the 6th Armored Division recommended that the Army switch to a mixture of two-thirds M4A3E2 and one-third 105mm howitzer tanks for the remainder of combat operations in 1945.

A white-washed M4A3E2 assault tank of the 743rd Tank Battalion while supporting the 30th Infantry Division in Malmedy, Belgium on January 13, 1945 during the Battle of the Bulge.

In December 1944, the AGF considered reopening production of the M4A3E2, but the ASF responded that to manufacture 500 to 1,000 new assault tanks would require production facilities that would not be ready until late 1945. In February 1945, the Armored Board recommended building a new assault tank on the M4 chassis but with an armor basis of 7in to 8in, new horizontal volute suspension, and a turret derived from the T26E3 tank. AGF rebuffed this idea, arguing that the T26E3 Pershing was entering service. Instead, AGF recommended the development of a T26 variant with heavier armor, which would lead to the T32 heavy tank described below.

In early January 1945, Eisenhower's headquarters telegraphed Washington that the "M4A3E2 assault tank has proved itself in combat and has been most favorably received. The [European] Theater has an immediate requirement for the maximum number that can be produced without materially reducing the flow of tanks to the Continent. These tanks must be armed with the 76mm gun and should have the best available floatation characteristics."

In February 1945, a program began to re-arm the M4A3E2 with the 76mm gun. This was an off-shoot of an earlier Third US Army program to re-equip 300 normal M4A3 75mm gun tanks with the 76mm gun. Although a pilot

In 1945, about a hundred M4A3E2 assault tanks were upgraded with the 76mm gun in place of the usual 75mm gun. This is a M4A3E2 (76mm) bumper number E-2 of E Company, 2/32nd Armored Regiment, 3rd Armored Division at the intersection of Venloerstraße and Spichernstraße during the fighting in Cologne, March 6, 1945.

The ultimate version of the M4A3E2 assault tank was the T33 mechanized flamethrower, intended for the Pacific War. This had a new turret fitted with both a 75mm gun on the left side and an E20-20 flamethrower on the right.

was converted and a small stockpile of 76mm guns collected, the program was canceled due to the growing availability of the standard M4A3 (76mm) tanks. So, the guns were used to re-arm the M4A3E2 assault tanks instead. The Third US Army used the conversion process as an opportunity to substitute a .50-cal. heavy machine gun for the normal co-axial .30-cal. light machine gun. There were never any plans to supply the M4A3E2 through Lend–Lease, though in 1945, at least one was provided to the First French Army from 6th Army Group stocks. The M4A3E2 served in dwindling numbers through the end of the war. Bradley's 12th Army Group later noted that "These tanks ... were amazingly successful in operation, taking punishment not possible with the standard M4 series tanks. In spite of the increased weight no extra suspension troubles occurred and the campaign ended with many of these tanks still in operation." The M4A3E2 was essentially the US Army's infantry tank, similar in role to the British Churchill.

The AGF planned to make the M4A3E2 available for the final invasion of Japan. Ideally, the tank units in the Pacific wanted an assault tank armed with a flamethrower. As a result, the Chemical Weapons Service adapted the existing POA-CWS-H5 tank flamethrower as the E20-20 for a modified M4A3E2 variant. Rather than simply re-arm existing tank turrets, a new turret was developed for the M4A3E2 flamethrower tank that was subsequently designated as the Mechanized Flame Thrower T33. The T33 carried both an E20 flame gun as a co-axial weapon to the 75mm gun in the turret and also had an auxiliary E12R4 flame gun in the bow machine gun position in the hull. Three pilots were built on existing M4A3E2 tanks, and plans were underway to build 300 new T33 assault tanks starting in January 1946. By the time the war ended, the T33 was considered the most advanced US flame tank design, but the construction contracts were canceled at the end of the war with no serial production taking place.

T28 SUPER-HEAVY TANK

The largest and heaviest tank ever developed in the United States was the unusual T28 super-heavy tank. The design began in the summer of 1943 based on reports from the military attaché in Moscow, who forwarded information about a new German armored vehicle that had appeared at the Battle of Kursk. Although the Tiger heavy tank was already known from contact in Tunisia, the Ferdinand 88mm tank destroyer was new. Its frontal armor was reported to be 8in (203mm) thick, impervious to any American tank gun.

The new T28 heavy tank was expected to be turretless with 8in frontal armor (203mm), a 105mm gun derived from an experimental anti-aircraft gun, and a powertrain based on the T23 medium tank using an electric transmission similar to that on the M6A2 heavy tank. This was subsequently changed to the powertrain of the M26, tank due to Army resistance to the maintenance burden of the T23 tank's electric drive. Based on a 500hp engine, this gave the T28 a maximum road speed of 8mph, but a maximum sustained speed of only 7mph. Curiously enough, the British Army started its own A39 Tortoise project at this time with very similar requirements.

Ordnance wished to embark on a fast-paced development to enable the initial production batch of 25 tanks to be ready by the time that the US Army landed in France in the spring or fall of 1944. The tactical mission of the T28 was the engagement of German bunkers along the Westwall as described in an Ordnance letter:

The T28 super-heavy tank Pilot No. 1 on display at the Patton Museum at Fort Knox, in the 1980s. (Author)

> This self-propelled gun would be of great value in attacking German West Wall fortifications, since the gun would be capable of penetrating approximately 7in of armor plate or 6ft of concrete with a single shot at 500yds range. It would be almost impossible to knock out this tank, due to the thickness and slope of the armor, except perhaps by a lucky shot near the ground which might break the track. The track, however, is very well protected and enclosed in side armor to the greatest possible extent.

The T28 heavy tank requirement proceeded through bureaucratic channels. The Chief of Ordnance, Gladeon Barnes, knew that AGF would not support the development of such a vehicle in view of the lack of "battle-need." Battle-need was the policy of Lt Gen. Lesley McNair, chief of AGF, who argued that new weapons had to be initiated by requests from commanders in the combat theaters, and not the "mad scientists" at labs in the United States. To skirt around this obstacle, on August 27, 1943 Barnes wrote directly to the head of ASF, Gen. Brehon B. Somervell, since ASF controlled weapons production. He outlined the general characteristics of the new tank and sought approval for an immediate order for 25 vehicles. Gen. Lucius Clay, the Director of Materiel at ASF, agreed to Barnes' request.

Barnes' attempt to maneuver around the AGF roadblock caused further delays in early 1944. The AGF responded to Barnes' bureaucratic maneuvers by complaining to Maj. Gen. Waldron, the Army's Assistant Chief of Staff for Requirements, that Ordnance was circumventing the usual development process and trying to start production of 25 tanks under the guise of pilot tanks without the suitable development and

 T28 ATTACK

The T28 super-heavy tank never saw combat, but what if …? This illustration shows a notional confrontation between a colorful marked T28 super-heavy tank and a Japanese O-I super-heavy tank during a battle in the Japanese Home Islands. The T28 has some combat modifications including late-war smoke mortars and the T1 Skink self-protection device, a miniature multi-shot flamethrower intended to protect tanks against short-range Japanese lunge mine attacks.

T95 105mm self-propelled gun Pilot No. 1 at APG, March 1946. The two cranes on either end of the superstructure were used to assist in the detachment of the suspension modules.

testing. In response, on March 19, 1944, Waldron cut back the initial phase of the program to three pilot tanks. Barnes pointed out to Waldron that the idea of building 24 tanks immediately was based on an Ordnance study that concluded that 24 tanks could be built in the same time as the three pilots, but if the ASF decided to order three pilots followed by an order for more tanks at some later date, the second batch would not be available for a further 18 to 24 months. Waldron agreed to increase the size of the pilot program to five tanks, but resisted Barnes' plea for two dozen tanks without prior testing.

In July, Gen. Clay challenged Barnes again over the weight increases on the T28 after recent Ordnance documents suggested it had ballooned from 80 to 95 tons. This put a temporary hold on the program until Ordnance could explain how it would restrain the size growth of the tank. Weight-cutting efforts were put in place, though in fact the combat-loaded weight of the T28 eventually crept back up to 90 tons.

With senior Army approval begrudgingly granted, Ordnance sought a firm that could handle such an unusually large vehicle. The most likely candidate, BLW, balked on the grounds that it was already heavily committed to numerous tank manufacture programs and could not spare the resources without impacting higher priority programs. Ordnance eventually selected Paccar (Pacific Car and Foundry), issuing it a $1,128,000 contract in July 1944 for the five pilots. As a consequence of the numerous delays, Barnes' plan to field the T28 heavy tank by the summer of 1944 had evaporated.

Even if the T28 had been ready in 1944, it is hard to see whether its role in attacking enemy fortifications was worth the extreme effort it would have required to transport it to Europe and deploy it in the terrain and road conditions along the German Westwall. The US Army fought along the Westwall starting in September 1944 and did not face insurmountable problems dealing with its bunkers. Many of them had been stripped of guns and armored embrasures in 1943–44 to equip the Atlantic Wall. One of the most effective weapons in dealing with the Westwall bunkers was the M12 155mm GMC. This was based on the Sherman tank chassis, so it was much

An overhead view of T95 105mm self-propelled gun Pilot No. 1 at APG, March 1946.

easier to deploy than the T28. It was not as well armored, but its 155mm gun was significantly more powerful than the 105mm gun on the T28, so it could be used from stand-off distances. The T28 super-heavy tank was an extravagant over-reaction to the threat of German fortified strongpoints. It was too slow and clumsy for typical battlefield engagements.

By August 1944, the basic drawings for the T28 heavy tank had been completed. A set had been forwarded to the Corps of Engineers to permit it time to develop suitable ferrying and bridging equipment, since the T28 was so much heavier and wider than any previous tank. Ordnance also initiated work on a "wet ferrying" system that would have consisted of pontoons attached to the T28 to permit it to cross river obstacles. However, this effort was canceled when the Engineers pointed out the problems in developing such systems for much smaller tanks such as the M4 medium tank.

Due to the lack of a turret on the T28, the 105mm T5E1 gun was provided with limited traverse of 10 degrees to either side as well as elevation from minus 10 to plus 20 degrees. The gun mounting was developed by Chevrolet Motor Company. In view of its unusual size, the castings for the T28 were not ready until February 1945. Another novel feature of the T28 was the suspension. In order to keep ground pressure within reasonable limits, it was necessary to use exceptionally wide tracks. The solution to this problem was to mount two separate sets of tracks and bogies on either side of the hull. This would have made the T28 too wide to transport by railroad or ship, so the next solution was to encapsulate the outer suspension set as a detachable module. The two outer sets could be readily detached from the tank, towed behind it, and then reattached once reaching the combat theater. Each suspension set weighed 24 tons, due to its side armor, so this accounted for about half of the tank's overall weight. It took about four hours for the crew to detach the outer track assembly, and about the same time to re-assemble it back on the tank. The suspension bogies were derived from the new Sherman HVSS bogie, as was the track.

After being detached from the T28 tank, the suspension modules could be linked together and towed behind the tank.

In May 1948, Ordnance tested the transportability of the T28 using Landing Ship Tank LST-1128 on Chesapeake Bay, Maryland. During this test, the width of the T28 had been reduced by removing the two suspension modules.

A cross-sectional view of the T28 Super-Heavy Tank.

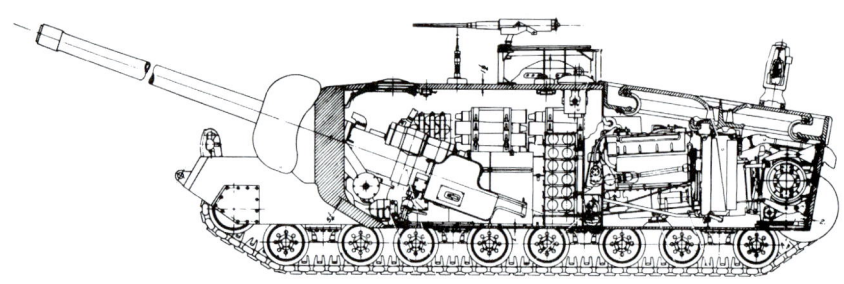

Super-heavy tank armor comparison		
	Maus	T28
Gun mantlet	220mm @ 60° = 254mm	292mm^
Turret front	220mm^	n/a
Turret sides	210mm @ 60° = 243mm	n/a
Hull front	200mm @ 40° = 311mm	305mm
Hull sides (upper)	185mm	64mm @ 23° = 117mm
Hull sides (lower)	185mm	152mm

^ = curved armor

In February 1945, Barnes suggested that the T28 be renamed from a heavy tank to a gun motor carriage, since it lacked a turret as well as the usual co-axial and hull machine guns. This was approved in March 1945 by the Ordnance Committee as the T95 105mm Gun Motor Carriage. However, in June 1946, it changed for the third and final time to T28 Super-Heavy Tank.

The Corps of Engineers remained unhappy about the T28/T95, due to both its heavy weight and its width. In March 1945, it inserted a formal statement into one of the progress reports that warned that the vehicle could only be moved across a river using an M4 floating bridge and only if the river currents were less than 9mph. Otherwise it would have to use a reinforced Bailey bridge, but only on spans of 110ft or less.

The first front hull castings were shipped to APG in May 1945. They successfully resisted fire from German 88mm and US 90mm guns from a range of 1,100yds (1,000m). The first production casting arrived at Paccar on June 20, 1945 and the first hull was completed in August 1945. Since the war against Japan had ended, Ordnance recommended reducing the number of pilots from five to two. Pilot No. 1 was completed late in 1945 and after preliminary trials, departed Paccar for APG on December 21, 1945. Pilot No. 2 was shipped to the Armored Board at Fort Knox on January 10, 1946.

E

T28 SUPER-HEAVY TANK, ABERDEEN PROVING GROUND, 1947
The T28 was simply marked, carrying its white registration number U.S.A. 40226809 on the superstructure side. It also carried its designation "Super-Heavy Tank T28" in chrome yellow on the forward superstructure, since this tank was frequently used for displays at the base. On the side is a chrome yellow square with a black No. 45, an APG test marking. The T28 was finished in the usual overall lusterless olive drab.

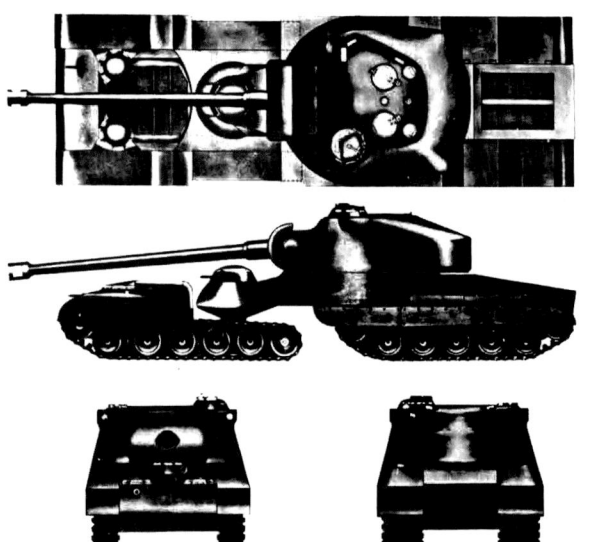

This peculiar semi-trailer tank was proposed by the Armored Medical Research Lab in 1945 in response to the AGF Equipment Review Board's recommendation for a future 150-ton super tank.

Tests of the two pilots were conducted through 1946. A final Ordnance report in 1947 concluded:

The increase in armor and weight without increase in power capacity critically reduced the mobility of the vehicle. The Super-Heavy T28 was considered unsatisfactory from the standpoints of mobility, reliability, and performance, although the 105mm gun T5E1 was found satisfactory. A series of component deficiencies were encountered. It was recommended that no further test work be conducted on this vehicle unless the need developed for such heavy vehicles.

During the testing of the second pilot at the Yuma Test Branch of the Engineer Board of the Corps of Engineers at Imperial Dam, Arizona in 1947, the engine caught fire. Due to the extent of the fire damage and the low priority of the program by this time, the second pilot was scrapped. The first pilot remained at APG for many years and eventually ended up at Fort Belvoir in Virginia in the Washington, DC suburbs. It was long thought to have been scrapped. Hidden under a mass of vines and weeds, it was rediscovered by tank buffs in 1974.

Heavy tank comparison: 1945				
Type	Maus	T28/T95	Tiger II	T29E3
Crew	5	4	5	6
Weight (tons: unloaded)	185	90.3	75.5	67.5
Length (ft)	33.1	36.5	33.8	37.9
Width (ft)	12.0	14.9	12.3	12.5
Height (ft)	12.0	9.3	10.1	10.6
Engine (hp)	1,100	500	690	770
Hp/ton ratio	5.9	5.5	9.1	11.4
Ground pressure (hp/ton)	20.0	11.7	10.8	12.4
Road speed (mph)	12.0	8	25.8	22
Main gun	128	105	88	105
Turret frontal armor (mm)	240	n/a	180	279
Turret side armor (mm)	200	n/a	80	127
Hull frontal armor (mm)	200	292	150	102
Hull side armor (mm)	180	152	80	76

T29, T30, AND T34 HEAVY TANKS

In 1942, Ordnance began work on the M4X program to develop an eventual successor to the M4 Sherman medium tank. This led to a series of designs, including the T20, T23, and T25, which examined alternative design approaches. In 1944, the T25 medium tank evolved into the T26 medium tank, but with heavier armor. It eventually emerged as the T26E3, better known by its standardized designation as the M26 Pershing. It was reclassified as a heavy tank in June 1944, but reverted to a medium tank classification in 1947. The M26 Pershing is not covered in this book due to its fluctuating designation as well as its extensive coverage in two other Osprey books.[2]

Late-war heavy tanks of 1945 size comparison (from right to left): US T29E3, German Tiger II (King Tiger), US T28, and German Maus.

The continual escalation of German tank firepower and armored protection led Ordnance to recommend the development of a more powerful tank than the eventual M26 Pershing. The intention was to create tanks that were as mobile as contemporary medium tanks but with more powerful guns and thicker armor. Two related designs were proposed, the T29 with a T5E2 105mm gun and the T30 with the T7 155mm gun. Frontal turret armor was 7in (178mm) and frontal hull armor was 4in (102mm). The program was approved on September 28, 1944 for the construction of pilot tanks. Pressed Steel Car (PSC) of Chicago, Illinois was awarded the contracts for their construction on November 22, 1944. The initial Army plan in March 1945 recommended a limited procurement of 1,200 T29 and 504 T30, but by April 1945 this was reduced to only 1,152.

The new heavy tanks bore a family resemblance to the M26 Pershing, but they were substantially larger and heavier. The initial plan was to power the T29 with a 700hp Ford GAC V-12 engine with a CD-850-1 cross-drive transmission. In order to accommodate the powerful new guns, the chassis had an 80in turret ring. Due to the size of the ammunition, there were four crew in the turret: the usual gunner and commander, but two loaders instead of the usual one. The T29 stowed 46 105mm rounds in the turret and 17 in the hull for a total of 63. In contrast, the T30 carried only 34 rounds due to their substantial size. In May 1945, Ordnance recommended that a third new tank gun, the T53 120mm gun, be fitted to the family as the T34 heavy tank.

Both the AGF and the Armored Board were unhappy about the trend towards such large and heavy tanks as summarized in a post-war report by the former:

Ordnance was approaching the problem from the wrong standpoint. It was the desire of [AGF] to develop better, but not necessarily bigger tanks; to arm these with harder-hitting but not necessarily bigger guns; to increase power and mobility without increasing unit ground pressure; and not to increase armor unless an increase in firepower was achieved without a significant increase in ground pressure.

Manufacture of the first T29 heavy tank pilot was completed shortly before the end of the war in August 1945, but the T30 pilot had only progressed as far as a wooden mock-up of the turret. The production contract for PSC was terminated after the end of the war. The pilots, drawings, and other

2 Steven Zaloga, *M26/M46 Pershing Tank 1943–53*, Osprey New Vanguard 35: 2000; Steven Zaloga, *Pershing vs Tiger: Germany 1945*, Osprey Duel 80: 2017.

The first pilot of the T29 heavy tank completed at PSC had a different engine deck from later tanks of the family, due to the use of the original Ford GAC engine. It initially lacked a muzzle brake for its 105mm gun.

associated material were transferred to the Detroit Arsenal.

In January 1945, AGF established an Equipment Review Board in Washington, DC to discuss future weapons needs. In June 1945, the board released its recommendations, calling for a heavy assault tank in the 75-ton range with a gun in excess of 90mm and frontal armor of 10.5in (267mm). The board also recommended a super tank for research purposes with a weight up to 150 tons. Unlike the existing T28/T95 program, the board suggested that the armament be mounted in a fully traversable turret. The board recognized the problems of transporting such a heavy vehicle, and so acknowledged that an unconventional modular tank might be required. The report included an illustration of a model of a "semi-trailer" tank configuration designed by an officer of the Armored Medical Research Lab as a possible concept.

Following the war, Allied troops discovered evidence of the German super-heavy tanks such as the E-100 and the Maus. On September 7, 1945, the Allies staged a victory parade in Berlin where the Red Army displayed its new IS-3 heavy tank for the first time. Its sleek hemispherical turret and sharply angled bow armor were a shock to American and British observers. There was some concern that its armor would be proof against existing tank guns. The US Army had managed to locate several IS-2 heavy tank wrecks in the rubble of Berlin and to ship parts back to APG for evaluation.

A T29E1 heavy tank being tested on the new heavy tank transporter combination of the T79 100-ton 10-wheel trailer and T29 20-ton tractor truck. The T29E1 tank used the Continental AV-1790-3 engine and so had a revised engine deck compared to the first T29 with a Ford GAC engine.

A T29E3 pilot at the Patton Museum at Fort Knox in the 1980s. The T29E3 program reconfigured T29 tank No. 8 with a T31E1 rangefinder, evident from the extension on the side of the turret. (Author)

In November 1945, the War Department convened its own Equipment Review Board, headed by Gen. Joseph Stillwell. Its report was released in January 1946 and concurred with the AGF about the need for a new heavy tank, but it did not support a new super-heavy tank.

Despite the war's end, Ordnance recommended that the program continue to serve as the basis for future tank development. This was reinforced by the discovery of the new German and Soviet heavy tanks. The foreign developments also elicited some interest from US firms involved in wartime tank production. At a May 1946 conference at the Armored School at Fort Knox, Chrysler Corporation displayed a model of a proposed 60-ton "K Tank" fitted with a hemispherical turret reminiscent of the Soviet IS-3, but with the turret mounted unconventionally at the rear of the hull. This futuristic design also placed the entire crew in the turret, including the driver. The K Tank failed to receive any support from the US Army, in large measure due to the heavy cuts in research funding after the war.

On August 23, 1945, the Army approved the construction of ten T29 and 12 T30 heavy tanks at the Detroit Arsenal. This was amended in November 1946 to divert two of the T30 pilots to the T34 configuration with the 120mm gun. All of these pilots were assigned to Detroit Arsenal for manufacturing. During the manufacture, Ordnance decided to substitute the Continental AV-1790-3 engine on the T29 Pilot No. 1, redesignating it as T29E1.

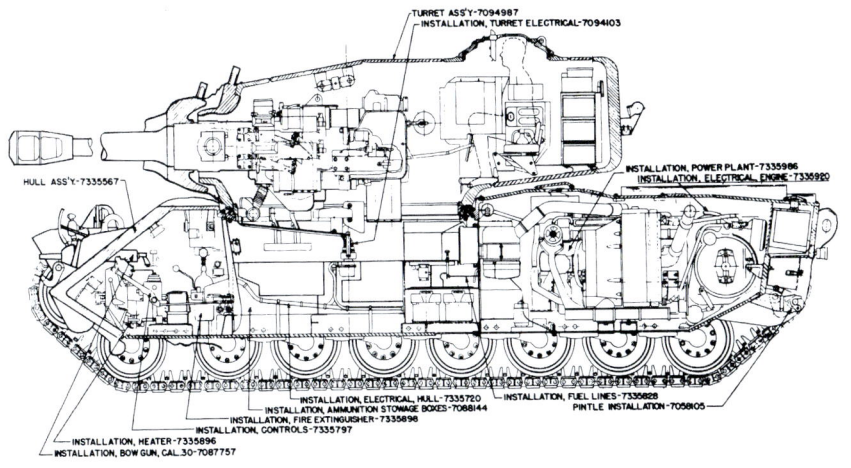

A T29 cross-section showing the original configuration with the Ford GAC V-12 engine.

A T30 heavy tank preserved for many years at the APG.

T29 Pilot No. 2 received a new turret stabilization system developed at the Massachusetts Institute of Technology. This was designated as the T29E2 in April 1948. Due to the end of the war, there was no urgency in the completion of these programs, so the pilots were not delivered for service trials until early 1948.

The first set of trails at the Army Field Forces Board at Fort Knox had a very mixed reaction to the T29 and T30 pilot tanks. They were both considered automotively unsatisfactory, due to transmission overheating. In addition, the designs were not well suited to maintenance, due to the difficulty of removing the engine and transmission for repair. After improvements were made, three T29 and two T30 heavy tanks were subjected to a further round of automotive tests at APG, with continuing tests at Fort Knox. The heavy tanks were considered to have many desirable features, but their automotive design remained troublesome.

Heavy tank gun performance

	105mm	120mm	155mm
Tank	T28, T29, T32	T34	T30
Gun	T5	T53	T7
HE projectile	T30E1	M73	M107
Projectile weight (lb)	33.5	49.6	95.0
Velocity (ft/sec)	3,100	3,097	2,352
APCBC projectile	T32	T14E3	T43
Projectile weight (lb)	39.0	49.8	100.0
Velocity (ft/sec)	3,000	3,150	2,533
Armor pen (mm)*	135	210	220
HVAP projectile	T29E3	T17E1	T35
Projectile weight (lb)	24.6	35.9	57.2
Velocity (ft/sec)	3,700	3,550	3,630
Armor pen (mm)	251	276	262

*@1,000yds at 30 degrees obliquity

The 105mm and 120mm guns in the T29 and T30 were the most powerful weapons ever mounted in a US tank. However, they were not capable of reliably penetrating the frontal armor of either the German Tiger II or Soviet IS-3 at long range until new shaped-charge HEAT (high-explosive anti-tank) or HESH (high-explosive squash-head) ammunition was developed.

T29E3 HEAVY TANK, ABERDEEN PROVING GROUND, 1949
The T29E3 was very simply marked, carrying its registration number U.S.A. 30162841 on the fender tool stowage bin. The tank was finished in standard lusterless olive drab.

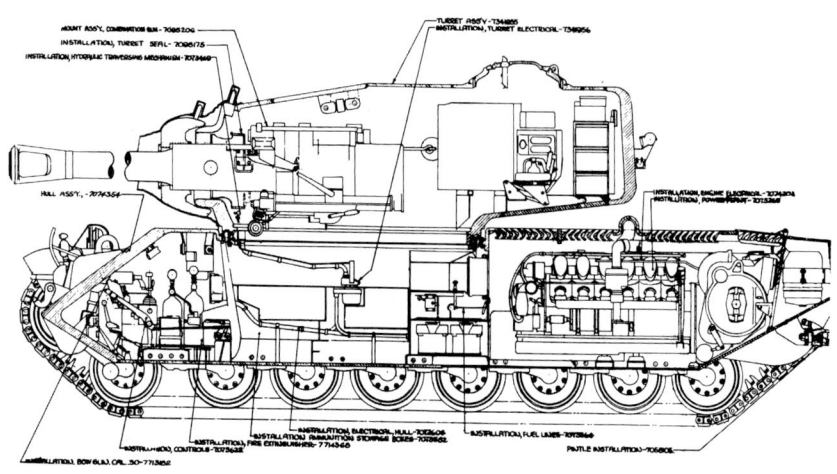

An Armored Board report summarized the effectiveness of the 105mm and 155mm guns against the Tiger II and IS-3:

Neither of the two guns under consideration can be expected to defeat the front plate of the [Tiger II] or [IS-3] at any reasonable range irrespective of the directness of angle-of-attack. The 3-inch [76mm] hull side of the [Tiger II] inclined at only 25 degrees is overmatched by both projectiles and should be vulnerable throughout a wide choice of angle and range of attack. The upper hull side of the [IS-3] is 90mm inclined at 45 degrees and is therefore considerably less vulnerable to the two guns in question respecting both angle-of-attack and range. Lower hull sides are of the order of 3-inches placed vertically on both [Tiger II and IS-3], hence these particular areas present no problem to either gun. The turret front and sides of the [Tiger II] turret are about 7.5 [190mm] and 3.5 inches [89mm] respectively. Thus either gun can expect to defeat the turret side even at fairly long range. However, it is estimated that only at ranges of the order of 1,000 yards or less can the main armament of Heavy Tanks T29 and T30 consistently defeat the turret front of [Tiger II]. The 200mm turret front of [IS-3] is well rounded and presents a very difficult target for either gun. The turret sides, if 200mm, would be equally as difficult to defeat as the turret front[3] ... then the task of penetrating is not likely of attainment by either gun under consideration irrespective of range or angle of attack. ... All-around performance of the 155m Gun, T7, in Heavy Tank T30 appears to be generally superior to that of the 105mm Gun, T5E2 on Heavy Tank T29. However, this superiority is restricted to high explosive shell effectiveness and to a potential advantage contingent on use of [future] shaped charge [HEAT] and [HESH] shells not currently available. There is essentially no notable difference in penetrating ability for the two guns firing HVAP [high-velocity armor-piercing] ammunition at ranges of 2,000 yards.

Both the US Army and US Marine Corps felt that a 70-ton heavy tank was excessive and would be difficult to deploy overseas. Most cargo

---

3 The actual thickness of the IS-3 turret was somewhat thinner than the US intelligence estimates, varying from 110mm to 220mm.

ships of the time were limited to 50-ton cranes, so unloading could only be undertaken in ports with heavy dockside cranes. Furthermore, there was a distinct shortage of railroad flatcars capable of hauling 70-ton loads. In the United States at the time, only 3.4 percent of flatcars could handle 70-ton loads. There were no 70-ton flatcars available in Europe at the time, according to US assessments. In response to these concerns, in December 1948, Ordnance recommended that the T34 heavy tank with 120mm gun be reconfigured with a shorter hull, lighter 120mm gun, and a more refined armor design. This was expected to reduce the weight to 58 tons.

The T34 heavy tank employed the T53 120mm gun, but it was otherwise similar to the rest of the T29/T30 heavy tank family.

Ordnance undertook a series of upgrades to the pilot heavy tanks to improve their performance and to examine technologies suitable for future heavy tanks. T29 Pilot No. 8 was fitted with the new T136 mount that included a T31E1 wide-base optical rangefinder and T93E2 telescope. This was very evident on the turret, since the rangefinder required large housings on either side of the turret to accommodate the range finder. This configuration was developed to explore future integrated fire control systems, and the resulting design was designated as the T29E3 heavy tank.

The ammunition for the 155mm gun on the T30 weighed 135lb consisting of a 95lb high-explosive projectile and separate 40lb propellant charge. To accelerate reloading, the T30E1 was modified to incorporate a power ammunition lifting device, an automatic ammunition ramming mechanism, an automatic ejection system for the spent propellant case, and a drive mechanism to return the gun to its original position following the loading/firing sequence.

The final test report on the T29 and T30 at APG in early 1950 concluded that "because of numerous mechanical deficiencies of the power plants and suspensions, the vehicles were considered unsuitable. The performance ability of the T29 was superior to that of the T30." The assorted heavy tank pilots remained at the proving grounds for several years, mainly as testbeds for their guns in support of other programs. In their place, the T43 program proceeded to standardization and entered serial production in 1953 as the M103 heavy tank.[4]

4   Kenneth Estes, *M103 Heavy Tank 1950–74*, Osprey New Vanguard 197: 2017.

 T30 HEAVY TANK, ABERDEEN PROVING GROUND, 1948

The T30 Pilot No. 1 carried very simple markings, including the registration number U.S.A. 30102842 on the side of the fender stowage bin and some identification stenciling on the turret side. It was finished in overall lusterless olive drab.

1

2

THE T32 ASSAULT TANK

Although sharing a test number in the same sequence as other late-war US heavy tanks, the T32 was developed separately as an assault tank to replace the wartime M4A3E2. This program began in December 1944 by improving the armor of the existing T26E3 as the T26E5. However, in February 1945, Ordnance proposed a more elaborate program using Pershing tank components. This was in part a response to the AGF's criticism of the T29 and T30 heavy tanks.

The construction of four pilots of the new T32 heavy tank was approved, and Chrysler was assigned to the program. Unlike the T29 and T30 that used enlarged turrets, the T32 turret was patterned after the Pershing turret, but with much thicker armor. The turret armor varied from 11.7in (298mm) to 6in (152mm) on the rear. The front hull armor was 5in (127mm) at 54 degrees, giving it the equivalent of 217mm. The powertrain for the T32 was the same as for the T29 heavy tank, but the hull was extended by adding an additional road-wheel station on both sides. The T32 was armed with the T15E2 90mm gun, a lengthened version of the 90mm gun on the M26 Pershing. It had seen limited combat use in 1945 on a single "Super-Pershing" that had been deployed with the 3rd Armored Division in Germany on an experimental basis.

The first two T32 pilots were completed by April 1946 and sent to APG for trials. The second batch used rolled plate armor on the front instead of cast, and the bow machine gun station was deleted. As a result, Pilots 3 and 4 were designated as T32E1. These were completed by June 1946 with Pilot No. 3 sent to Fort Knox and Pilot No. 4 remaining at the Detroit Arsenal for testing. These tanks used the early EX-120 cross-drive transmission, but this subsequently proved to be a major source of problems during the automotive trials. The March 1949 APG report on its trials concluded that "The performance characteristics of the test vehicle were considered excellent for its weight class. Operation of the vehicle was limited by the poor reliability of its transmission." Despite its favorable

Chrysler displayed this wooden model of its proposed K Tank at the Armored School in May 1946. Not only did it have a rear-mounted turret with 105mm gun, but it was armed with two subsidiary .50-cal. heavy machine gun turrets at the rear in unusual elevating mounts for anti-aircraft defense. (AHEC)

test report, the T32 program faded away in the early 1950s with the pilot tanks used for various trials.

US HEAVY TANKS IN RETROSPECT

The US Army fielded only two heavy tanks in World War II, the M4A3E2 assault tank and the M26 Pershing heavy tank. Arguably, neither tank fits comfortably in the heavy tank category. The M4A3E2 was a medium tank with reinforced armor. The M26 was originally considered a medium tank, reclassified for a time as a heavy tank, and then reverted back to the medium tank classification after the war.

Both tanks were welcomed into combat service, since they both addressed specific tactical needs. The M4A3E2 recognized the infantry need for a breakthrough tank better protected against the ubiquitous German anti-tank gun of the day, the 75mm PaK 40. US tank armor had failed to advance from 1941 to 1944, even though the Germans consistently increased their anti-tank firepower from the 37mm gun of 1939 to the 50mm gun of 1941 and the 75mm gun of 1943. The Armored Force had been focused on its armored divisions from 1941 to 1943 and gave the separate tank battalions little attention. The M4 Sherman was well suited to the exploitation role of the armored divisions, but arguably was not as well suited to the infantry support role of the separate tank battalions where better armor would have

The Chrysler K Tank was a futuristic concept with a rear-mounted turret and the crew located in the turret. (AHEC)

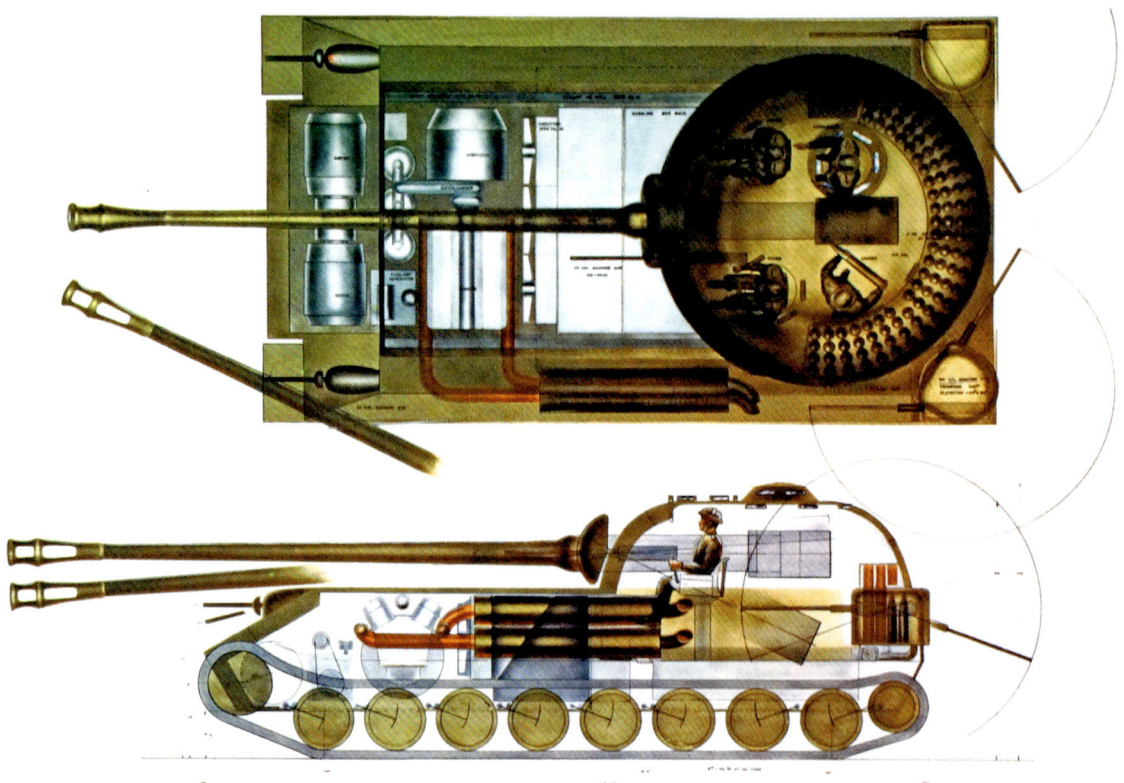

been welcome. The M4A3E2 was a last-minute recognition of this issue, but it was never built in adequate numbers, due to resistance from Ordnance that favored its own heavy tank designs.

The M26 Pershing with its 90mm gun was needed to deal with the heavier armor of German tanks, notably the Panther. The main problem with the M26 Pershing was that it arrived in combat too late, in February 1945 instead of February 1944. The complex reasons for this are outside the scope of this book, but are detailed in other books in the Osprey New Vanguard series. The main problem was the failure of both the AGF and Ordnance to anticipate future threats in 1943 and have a solution in the field by the summer of 1944.

The M6 heavy tank was a failure at many levels. It was created to fight on the World War I battlefield against enemy machine gun nests and pillboxes. Its main drawback was its weight and size, which made it difficult to transport from the United States to combat theaters in Europe and the Pacific. This was a recurring obstacle for all US heavy tanks. Neither its armor nor firepower justified its extravagant weight and size. Its armament was archaic on the 1943 battlefield if compared to the 88mm gun on the Tiger I. The Tiger I was designed in response to the appearance of the Soviet T-34 and KV tanks in 1941. As a result, it was armed with a gun powerful enough to destroy enemy heavy tanks and armor sufficient to shield itself against contemporary anti-tank guns. The M6 was not well enough armed to deal with German tanks such as the Tiger and Panther, nor was its armor proof against typical German anti-tank weapons of 1943–44.

The T14 assault tank was a fluke, developed solely for a British requirement. It would have been a good alternative to the M4A3E2, but it arrived on the scene too late for consideration, due to the low priority afforded to its development program.

The late-war heavy tanks were transitional designs. They arrived too late to enter combat. They would have been a formidable opponent to the German Tiger II (King Tiger), but it is questionable whether this mission

The T32 heavy tank Pilot No. 1, APG, March 1946, shortly after its delivery. As can be seen, it was much closer in configuration to the M26 Pershing tank than the T29/T30 heavy tanks.

The T32E1 pilot on the right with its turret reversed, parked next to a T30 heavy tank. The T32E1 used rolled armor plate for the bow instead of the casting used on the initial T32, and it lacked the bow machine gun. As can be seen, the T32 had a squatter turret than the T29/T30 series.

was worth the trouble in view of the tiny number of Tigers encountered by the US Army during the war. They remained in development into the late 1940s due to the perceived threat of tanks such as the Soviet IS-3 and its potential follow-ons. They never reached production since they were unnecessarily large. The eventual US heavy tank of the 1950s, the M103, was an evolutionary offshoot based on their technology. But the M103 was intentionally smaller with a better armor layout.

FURTHER READING

Richard Hunnicutt's book *Firepower* is the only significant study of US heavy tank development. It is highly recommended. G. MacLeod Ross' book provides the perspective of a member of the British Tank Mission in Washington, DC during the war years and contains several interesting notes on the British views of US heavy tanks. There are several internal Ordnance Department histories of wartime tank development that provide an essential source of information on the development of heavy tanks; these are located in the Ordnance files in Record Group 165 at the National Archives and Records Administration in College Park, Maryland. The Joseph Colby collection at the Ridgway Library of the US Army Heritage and Education Center in Carlisle, Pennsylvania contains a modest amount of correspondence about heavy tank development as well as some unique photographs.

Government reports and studies

Army Ground Forces Equipment Review Board: Board Study and Annexes, Army Ground Forces: December 1945

Development History of the 105mm Gun Motor Carriage T95 (Formerly Heavy Tank T28), Ordnance Department: April 1945

Development Record in Combat Vehicles, Ordnance Department: 1948

First Report on Assault Tank T14, Ordnance Research Center, Aberdeen Proving Ground: February 1944

Heavy Tank M6 and M6A1, Technical Manual TM 9-721, War Department: February 1943

Heavy Tanks and Assault Tanks, Ordnance Department: July 1945

Report of Army Field Forces on Armor, Army Field Forces: February 1949

The Role of the Army Ground Forces in the Development of Equipment, Historical Section, Army Ground Forces: 1946

Tank-Automotive Research and Development Test Resumes, Ordnance Tank-Automotive Command: 1949

Books and articles

Charles Bogart, "Major General George Lynch and the Tank: 1937–1941", *AFV News*, Sep–Dec 2003, pp. 14–19

Richard Hunnicutt, *Firepower: A History of the American Heavy Tank*, Presidio, Novato: 1988

Robert Icks, *The M6 Heavy and M26 Pershing*, AFV Weapons Profile 32, Profile Publications, Windsor: 1971

G. MacLeod Ross, *The Business of Tanks 1933 to 1945*, Stockwell, Devon, UK: 1976

INDEX